# Productivity Action Guide
## *for Authors*

# 90 Days to a More Productive *You!*

## D'vorah Lansky, M.Ed.

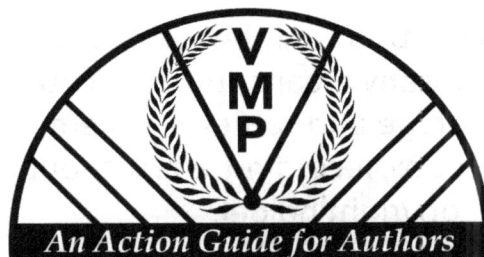

Vibrant Marketing Publications
Hartford, CT

Published by Vibrant Marketing Publications
Copyright ©2015 D'vorah Lansky

www.ActionGuidesForAuthors.com

All rights reserved. No part of this book may be reproduced
or transmitted in any form or by any means, including but
not limited to information storage and retrieval systems,
electronic, mechanical, photocopy, recording, etc. without
written permission from the copyright holder.

ISBN 978-0-9967431-0-5

# Dedication

This book is dedicated to my friend, colleague,
and journal publication coach, Kristen Joy.

Kristen, your brilliance has had a positive impact on
the lives of countless authors, includine mine!
Thank you for all you do.

It is a joy to be on this success journey with you!

# 90 Days to a More Productive *You!*

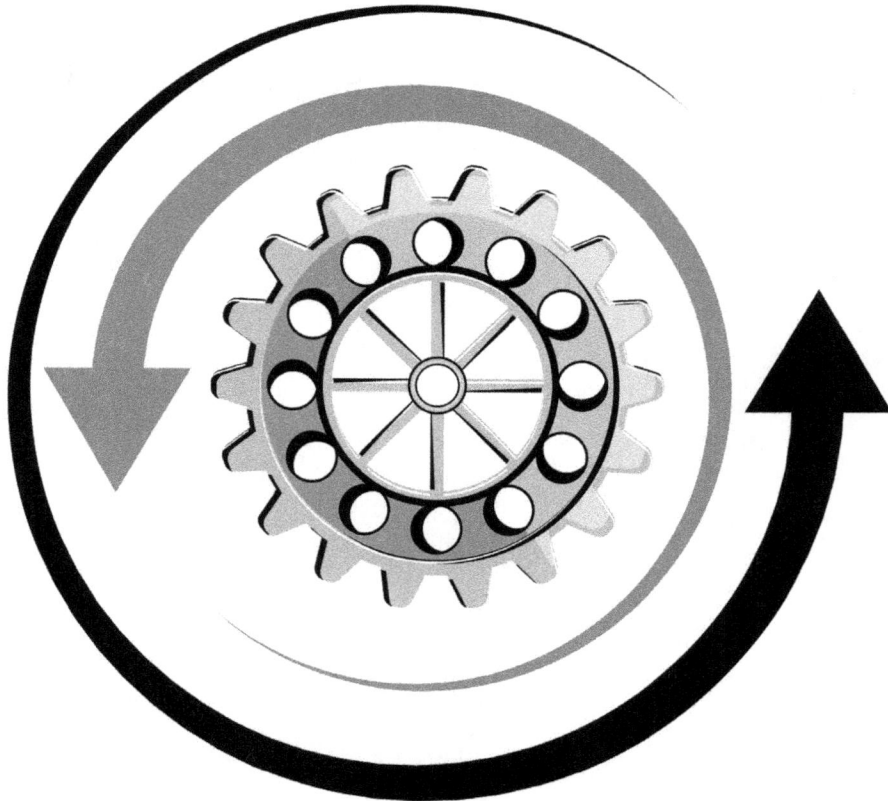

# Table of Contents

# How to Use This Action Guide

This action guide provides you with a 90-day road map for becoming more productive. To maximize your results, you'll want to take action and track your progress on a monthly, weekly, and daily basis. By tracking your activity and your results you will become more productive and this will propel you further along on your author success journey.

Each month, you'll have the opportunity to outline your goals, track your results, and establish a plan of action. Each week, you'll have opportunities to focus on specific projects, identify goals, create to-do lists, and journal your accomplishments.

In each of the monthly sections, you'll find four weekly sections. *For months where there is a fifth week, use that week to relax, reflect, and rejuvenate.*

**Description of Two Key Tracking Sheets Used in This Guide**

**Daily Six-Most-Important Things To-Do List:** It is likely that you have a to-do list a mile long. It would be impossible to accomplish everything on that list in one day. This can cause an author to feel overwhelmed or non-productive.

In this guide, you'll have the opportunity to prioritize your to-do list by selecting the six most important things to focus on each day. This will allow you to get more done while providing you with a sense of accomplishment.

**My Brain Dump Page:** This page provides you with a way to capture all of the ideas swimming around in your mind and all of the sticky notes and to-do lists floating around on your desk.

In this guide, you'll find one version of the "My Brain Dump Page" that includes the labels I use on my own brain dump pages. You'll also find a blank version called, "My Brain Dump Page for a Specific Project." You can use that page to help you focus on a specific project related to a success-focused goal for that month. Gather up all of your lists, notes, and ideas and plug them into your brain dump pages for that month.

Once you've filled in your brain dump pages, you'll have everything in one handy location. You can pull items from these pages to plug into your calendar or add to your "Daily Six-Most-Important Things To-Do List."

## Wishing you much success!

# Keeping Track of Books You Are Reading and Courses You Are Taking

| My Reading List | | |
|---|---|---|
| Author | Book Title | Date Completed |
| | | ☐ |
| | | ☐ |
| | | ☐ |
| | | ☐ |
| | | ☐ |
| | | ☐ |

| Courses I'm Taking or Courses I've Taken That Can Help Me Reach My Goals | | |
|---|---|---|
| Course Title | Website Address | Date Completed |
| | | ☐ |
| | | ☐ |
| | | ☐ |
| | | ☐ |
| | | ☐ |
| | | ☐ |

# Month One Section

# Notes

_____

_____

_____

_____

_____

_____

_____

_____

_____

_____

# Things to Focus on This Coming Month

Month: _____ Year: _____

My #1 most important success-focused goal for this month is: _____

_____

_____

_____

_____

Why I want to acheive this goal: _____

_____

_____

_____

_____

What my life will be like when I achieve this goal: _____

_____

_____

_____

_____

How my achieving this goal will impact others: _____

_____

_____

_____

_____

# Ways I Can Improve

What I commit to doing more of: _____

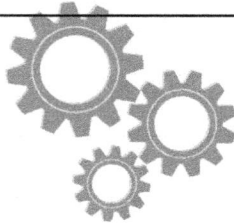

_____

_____

_____

_____

What I need to let go of: _____

_____

_____

_____

_____

What I need to do differently: _____

_____

_____

_____

_____

_____

# Monthly Calendar for: Month:_____ Year:_____

(Fill in the dates for this month then plug in tasks, events, and activities.)

| Monday | Tuesday | Wednesday | Thursday | Friday |
|--------|---------|-----------|----------|--------|
| | | | | |
| | | | | |
| | | | | |
| | | | | |
| | | | | |

13

# My Brain Dump Page

For the Month of: _____ Year: _____

| Business ASAP List | Personal ASAP List | Current Main Project |
|---|---|---|
| Speaking Activities | Writing Projects | Marketing Activities |
| Reading List | Courses to Study | To-Do Someday Maybe |

# My Brain Dump Page for a Specific Project

Project Description: _____

_____

# Notes

# Weekly Section for Month One

# My Main Focus for the Week of:_____

A Project I'll Be Focusing on This Week is: _____

_____

_____

_____

Why It's Important for Me to Focus on This Project This Week: _____

_____

_____

_____

## Master To-Do List for This Project

☐ _____     ☐ _____

☐ _____     ☐ _____

☐ _____     ☐ _____

☐ _____     ☐ _____

☐ _____     ☐ _____

☐ _____     ☐ _____

## How I'll Reward Myself to Celebrate My Accomplishments

_____

_____

_____

_____

# Daily Six-Most-Important Things To-Do List
## Week of: _____

| Notes: | Day of the Week: _____ |
|---|---|
| | ☐ _____ |
| Ways I'll market my book this week: | ☐ _____ |
| | ☐ _____ |
| | ☐ _____ |
| Something fun I'll do this week is: | ☐ _____ |
| | ☐ _____ |

| Day of the Week: _____ | Day of the Week: _____ |
|---|---|
| ☐ _____ | ☐ _____ |
| ☐ _____ | ☐ _____ |
| ☐ _____ | ☐ _____ |
| ☐ _____ | ☐ _____ |
| ☐ _____ | ☐ _____ |
| ☐ _____ | ☐ _____ |

| Day of the Week: _____ | Day of the Week: _____ |
|---|---|
| ☐ _____ | ☐ _____ |
| ☐ _____ | ☐ _____ |
| ☐ _____ | ☐ _____ |
| ☐ _____ | ☐ _____ |
| ☐ _____ | ☐ _____ |
| ☐ _____ | ☐ _____ |

# Journal

_____
_____
_____
_____
_____
_____
_____
_____

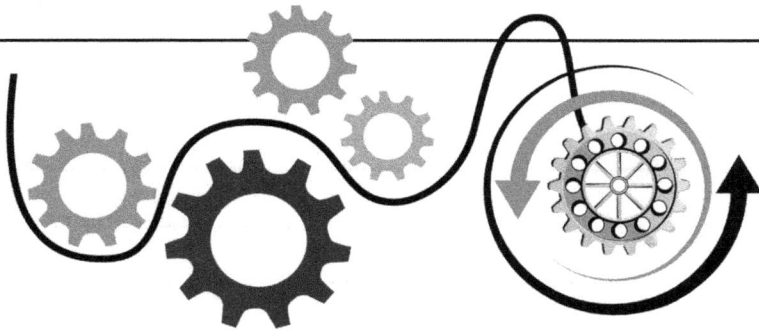

| What I Accomplished This Week | What I Will Get To Next Week |
|---|---|
| _____ | _____ |
| _____ | _____ |
| _____ | _____ |
| _____ | _____ |
| _____ | _____ |
| _____ | _____ |
| _____ | _____ |
| _____ | _____ |

# A Recap of My Week

The best part of my week: _____

_____

_____

_____

_____

### 5 Things I Learned This Week

○ _____
○ _____
○ _____
○ _____
○ _____

### 5 Things I Can Do To Be More Productive

○ _____
○ _____
○ _____
○ _____
○ _____

### 5 Things I'm Grateful For

○ _____
○ _____
○ _____
○ _____
○ _____

# Doodle - Brainstorm - Daydream

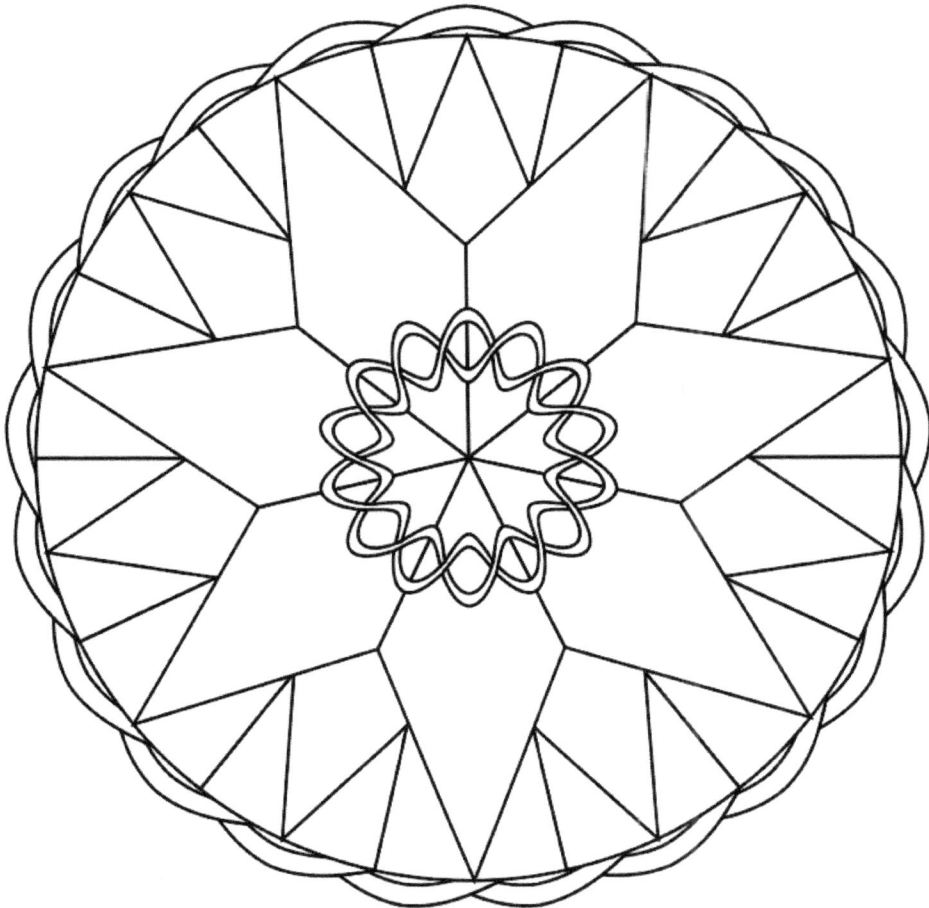

*"Productivity is never an accident. It is always the result of a commitment to excellence, intelligent planning, and focused effort."*
*—Paul J. Meyer*

# My Main Focus for the Week of:_____

A Project I'll Be Focusing on This Week is: _____

_____

_____

_____

Why It's Important for Me to Focus on This Project This Week: _____

_____

_____

_____

## Master To-Do List for This Project

☐ _____    ☐ _____

☐ _____    ☐ _____

☐ _____    ☐ _____

☐ _____    ☐ _____

☐ _____    ☐ _____

☐ _____    ☐ _____

## How I'll Reward Myself to Celebrate My Accomplishments

_____

_____

_____

_____

# Daily Six-Most-Important Things To-Do List
## Week of: _____

Notes:

Ways I'll market my book this week:

Something fun I'll do this week is:

Day of the Week: _____

- ☐ _____
- ☐ _____
- ☐ _____
- ☐ _____
- ☐ _____
- ☐ _____

Day of the Week: _____

- ☐ _____
- ☐ _____
- ☐ _____
- ☐ _____
- ☐ _____
- ☐ _____

Day of the Week: _____

- ☐ _____
- ☐ _____
- ☐ _____
- ☐ _____
- ☐ _____
- ☐ _____

Day of the Week: _____

- ☐ _____
- ☐ _____
- ☐ _____
- ☐ _____
- ☐ _____
- ☐ _____

Day of the Week: _____

- ☐ _____
- ☐ _____
- ☐ _____
- ☐ _____
- ☐ _____
- ☐ _____

# Journal

_____
_____
_____
_____
_____
_____
_____

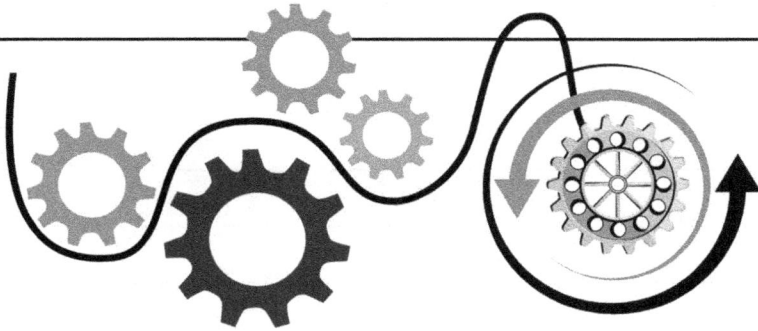

| What I Accomplished This Week | What I Will Get To Next Week |
|---|---|
| _____ | _____ |
| _____ | _____ |
| _____ | _____ |
| _____ | _____ |
| _____ | _____ |
| _____ | _____ |
| _____ | _____ |
| _____ | _____ |
| _____ | _____ |

# A Recap of My Week

The best part of my week: _____

_____

_____

_____

_____

### 5 Things I Learned This Week

○ _____

○ _____

○ _____

○ _____

○ _____

### 5 Things I Can Do To Be More Productive

○ _____

○ _____

○ _____

○ _____

○ _____

### 5 Things I'm Grateful For

○ _____

○ _____

○ _____

○ _____

○ _____

# Doodle - Brainstorm - Daydream

I LOVE TO WRITE
WRITE
I LOVE TO
I LOVE TO WRITE
I LOVE TO WRITE

*"If you think you can, you can.*
*And if you think you can't, you're right."*
—*Mary Kay Ash*

# My Main Focus for the Week of:_____

A Project I'll Be Focusing on This Week is: _____

_____

_____

_____

Why It's Important for Me to Focus on This Project This Week: _____

_____

_____

_____

## Master To-Do List for This Project

☐ _____    ☐ _____

☐ _____    ☐ _____

☐ _____    ☐ _____

☐ _____    ☐ _____

☐ _____    ☐ _____

☐ _____    ☐ _____

## How I'll Reward Myself to Celebrate My Accomplishments

_____

_____

_____

_____

# Daily Six-Most-Important Things To-Do List
## Week of: _____

Notes:

Ways I'll market my book this week:

Something fun I'll do this week is:

Day of the Week: _____

- ☐ _____
- ☐ _____
- ☐ _____
- ☐ _____
- ☐ _____
- ☐ _____

Day of the Week: _____

- ☐ _____
- ☐ _____
- ☐ _____
- ☐ _____
- ☐ _____
- ☐ _____

Day of the Week: _____

- ☐ _____
- ☐ _____
- ☐ _____
- ☐ _____
- ☐ _____
- ☐ _____

Day of the Week: _____

- ☐ _____
- ☐ _____
- ☐ _____
- ☐ _____
- ☐ _____
- ☐ _____

Day of the Week: _____

- ☐ _____
- ☐ _____
- ☐ _____
- ☐ _____
- ☐ _____
- ☐ _____

# Journal

_____
_____
_____
_____
_____
_____
_____

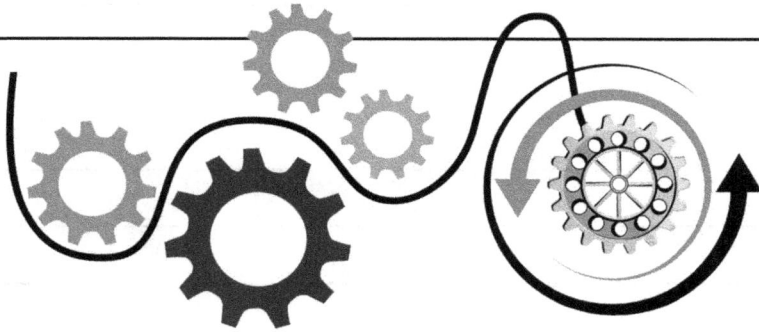

| What I Accomplished This Week | What I Will Get To Next Week |
| --- | --- |
| _____ | _____ |
| _____ | _____ |
| _____ | _____ |
| _____ | _____ |
| _____ | _____ |
| _____ | _____ |
| _____ | _____ |
| _____ | _____ |
| _____ | _____ |

# A Recap of My Week

The best part of my week: _____

_____

_____

_____

_____

### 5 Things I Learned This Week

○ _____

○ _____

○ _____

○ _____

○ _____

### 5 Things I Can Do To Be More Productive

○ _____

○ _____

○ _____

○ _____

○ _____

### 5 Things I'm Grateful For

○ _____

○ _____

○ _____

○ _____

○ _____

# Doodle - Brainstorm - Daydream

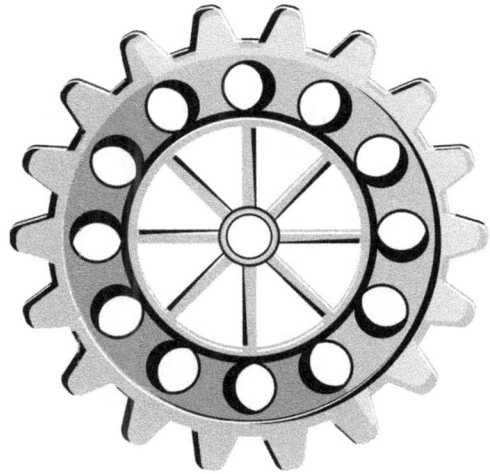

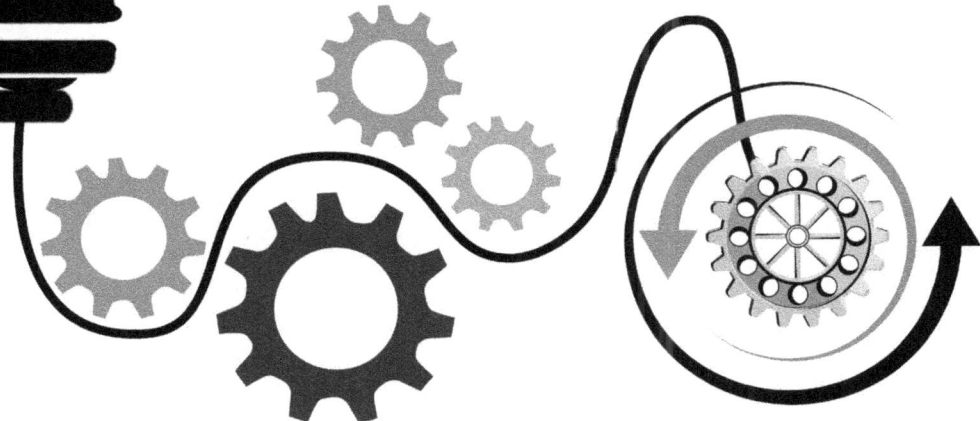

*"Opportunity is missed by most people because it is dressed in overalls and looks like work."*
*—Thomas A. Edison*

# My Main Focus for the Week of:_____

A Project I'll Be Focusing on This Week is: _____

_____

_____

_____

Why It's Important for Me to Focus on This Project This Week: _____

_____

_____

_____

## Master To-Do List for This Project

- [ ] _____  [ ] _____
- [ ] _____  [ ] _____
- [ ] _____  [ ] _____
- [ ] _____  [ ] _____
- [ ] _____  [ ] _____
- [ ] _____  [ ] _____

## How I'll Reward Myself to Celebrate My Accomplishments

_____

_____

_____

_____

# Daily Six-Most-Important Things To-Do List
## Week of: _____

| Notes: | Day of the Week: _____ |
|---|---|
| | ☐ _____ |
| | ☐ _____ |
| Ways I'll market my book this week: | ☐ _____ |
| | ☐ _____ |
| | ☐ _____ |
| Something fun I'll do this week is: | ☐ _____ |

| Day of the Week: _____ | Day of the Week: _____ |
|---|---|
| ☐ _____ | ☐ _____ |
| ☐ _____ | ☐ _____ |
| ☐ _____ | ☐ _____ |
| ☐ _____ | ☐ _____ |
| ☐ _____ | ☐ _____ |
| ☐ _____ | ☐ _____ |

| Day of the Week: _____ | Day of the Week: _____ |
|---|---|
| ☐ _____ | ☐ _____ |
| ☐ _____ | ☐ _____ |
| ☐ _____ | ☐ _____ |
| ☐ _____ | ☐ _____ |
| ☐ _____ | ☐ _____ |
| ☐ _____ | ☐ _____ |

# Journal

_____
_____
_____
_____
_____
_____

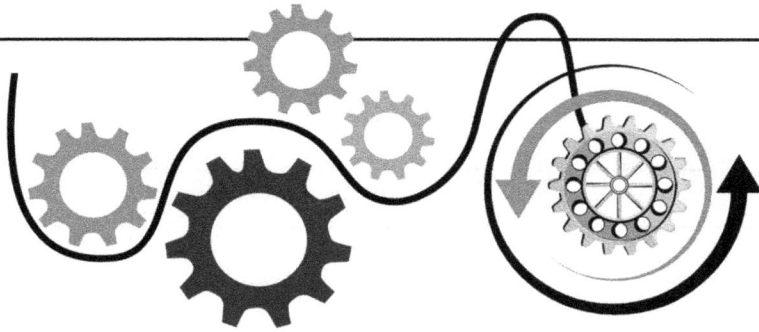

| What I Accomplished This Week | What I Will Get To Next Week |
|---|---|
| _____ | _____ |
| _____ | _____ |
| _____ | _____ |
| _____ | _____ |
| _____ | _____ |
| _____ | _____ |
| _____ | _____ |
| _____ | _____ |

# A Recap of My Week

The best part of my week: _____
_____
_____
_____
_____

### 5 Things I Learned This Week

○ _____
○ _____
○ _____
○ _____
○ _____

### 5 Things I Can Do To Be More Productive

○ _____
○ _____
○ _____
○ _____
○ _____

### 5 Things I'm Grateful For

○ _____
○ _____
○ _____
○ _____
○ _____

# Doodle - Brainstorm - Daydream

*"You must do the things you think you cannot do."*
*—Eleanor Roosevelt*

# Month Two
# Section

# Notes

_____

_____

_____

_____

_____

_____

_____

_____

_____

_____

## Things to Focus on This Coming Month

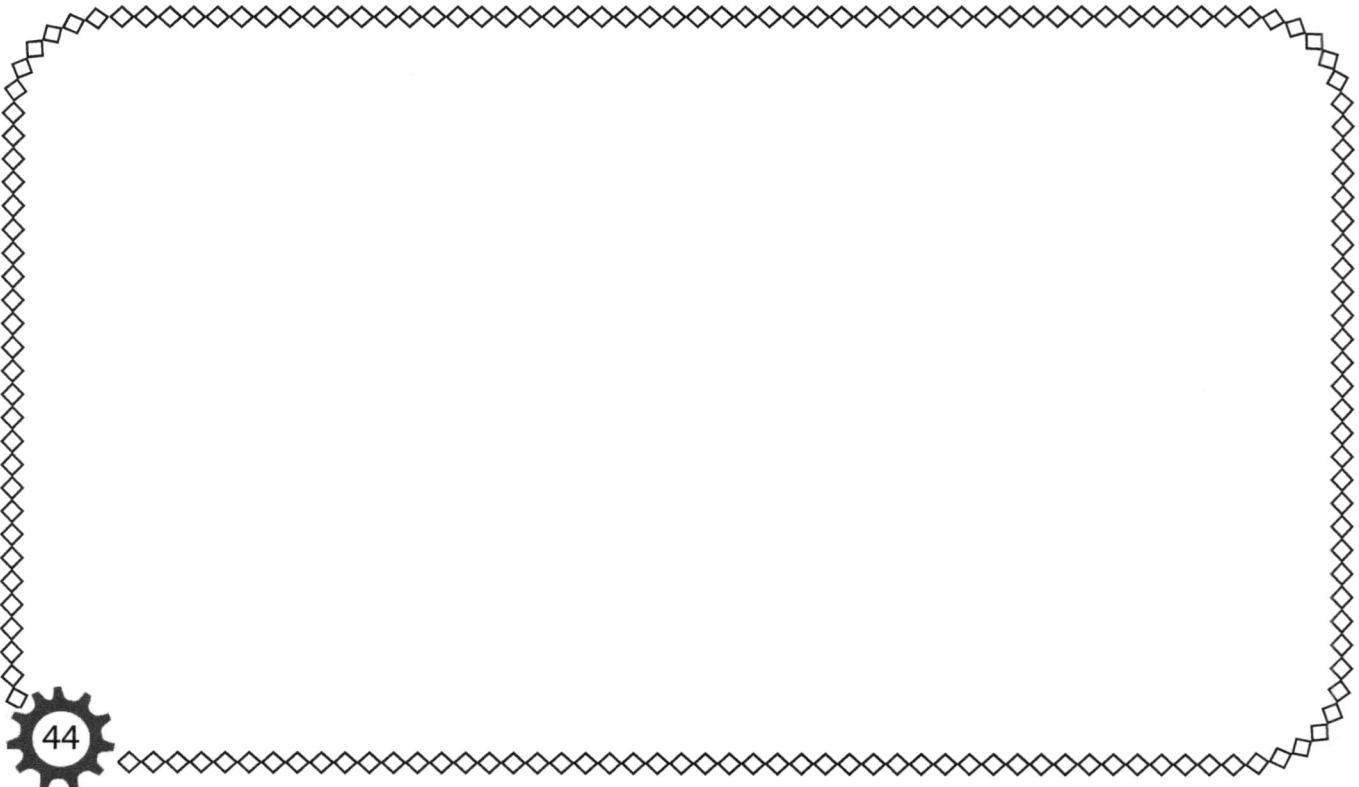

Month: _____ Year: _____

My #1 most important success-focused goal for this month is: _____

_____

_____

_____

_____

Why I want to acheive this goal: _____

_____

_____

_____

_____

What my life will be like when I achieve this goal: _____

_____

_____

_____

_____

How my achieving this goal will impact others: _____

_____

_____

_____

_____

# Ways I Can Improve

What I commit to doing more of: _____

_____

_____

_____

_____

What I need to let go of: _____

_____

_____

_____

_____

What I need to do differently: _____

_____

_____

_____

_____

# Monthly Calendar for: Month:_____ Year:_____

(Fill in the dates for this month then plug in tasks, events, and activities.)

| Monday | Tuesday | Wednesday | Thursday | Friday |
|--------|---------|-----------|----------|--------|
|        |         |           |          |        |
|        |         |           |          |        |
|        |         |           |          |        |
|        |         |           |          |        |
|        |         |           |          |   47   |

# My Brain Dump Page

For the Month of: _____ Year: _____

| Business ASAP List | Personal ASAP List | Current Main Project |
|---|---|---|
| | | |
| **Speaking Activities** | **Writing Projects** | **Marketing Activities** |
| | | |
| **Reading List** | **Courses to Study** | **To-Do Someday Maybe** |
| | | |

# My Brain Dump Page for a Specific Project

Project Description: _____

_____

# Notes

# Weekly Section for Month Two

# My Main Focus for the Week of:_____

A Project I'll Be Focusing on This Week is: _____
_____
_____
_____

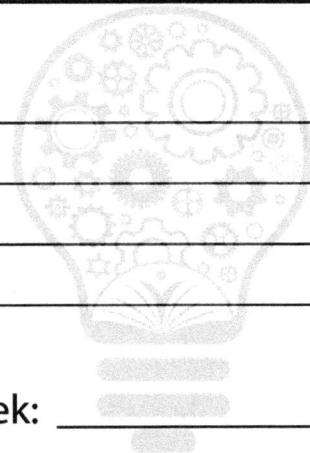

Why It's Important for Me to Focus on This Project This Week: _____
_____
_____
_____

## Master To-Do List for This Project

☐ _____    ☐ _____
☐ _____    ☐ _____
☐ _____    ☐ _____
☐ _____    ☐ _____
☐ _____    ☐ _____
☐ _____    ☐ _____

## How I'll Reward Myself to Celebrate My Accomplishments

_____
_____
_____
_____

# Daily Six-Most-Important Things To-Do List
## Week of: _____

Notes:

Ways I'll market my book this week:

Something fun I'll do this week is:

Day of the Week: _____

- ☐ _____
- ☐ _____
- ☐ _____
- ☐ _____
- ☐ _____
- ☐ _____

Day of the Week: _____

- ☐ _____
- ☐ _____
- ☐ _____
- ☐ _____
- ☐ _____
- ☐ _____

Day of the Week: _____

- ☐ _____
- ☐ _____
- ☐ _____
- ☐ _____
- ☐ _____
- ☐ _____

Day of the Week: _____

- ☐ _____
- ☐ _____
- ☐ _____
- ☐ _____
- ☐ _____
- ☐ _____

Day of the Week: _____

- ☐ _____
- ☐ _____
- ☐ _____
- ☐ _____
- ☐ _____
- ☐ _____

# Journal

_____

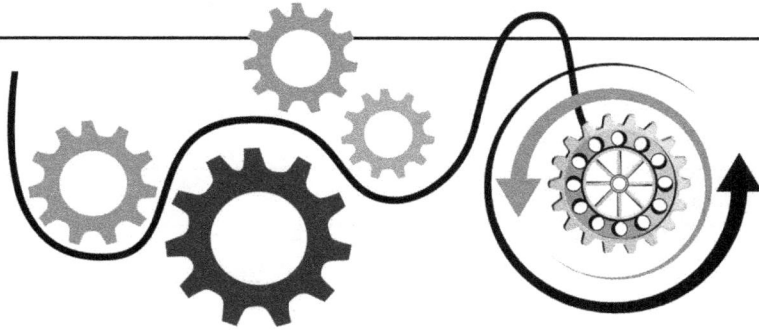

What I Accomplished
This Week

_____
_____
_____
_____
_____
_____
_____
_____

What I Will Get To
Next Week

_____
_____
_____
_____
_____
_____
_____
_____

# A Recap of My Week

The best part of my week: _____

_____

_____

_____

_____

### 5 Things I Learned This Week

○ _____

○ _____

○ _____

○ _____

○ _____

### 5 Things I Can Do To Be More Productive

○ _____

○ _____

○ _____

○ _____

○ _____

### 5 Things I'm Grateful For

○ _____

○ _____

○ _____

○ _____

○ _____

# Doodle - Brainstorm - Daydream

*"A goal is a dream with a deadline."*
*—Napoleon Hill*

# My Main Focus for the Week of:_____

A Project I'll Be Focusing on This Week is: _____

_____

_____

_____

Why It's Important for Me to Focus on This Project This Week: _____

_____

_____

_____

## Master To-Do List for This Project

☐ _____  ☐ _____

☐ _____  ☐ _____

☐ _____  ☐ _____

☐ _____  ☐ _____

☐ _____  ☐ _____

☐ _____  ☐ _____

## How I'll Reward Myself to Celebrate My Accomplishments

_____

_____

_____

_____

# Daily Six-Most-Important Things To-Do List
## Week of: _____

Notes:

Ways I'll market my book this week:

Something fun I'll do this week is:

Day of the Week: _____

- ☐ _____
- ☐ _____
- ☐ _____
- ☐ _____
- ☐ _____
- ☐ _____

Day of the Week: _____

- ☐ _____
- ☐ _____
- ☐ _____
- ☐ _____
- ☐ _____
- ☐ _____

Day of the Week: _____

- ☐ _____
- ☐ _____
- ☐ _____
- ☐ _____
- ☐ _____
- ☐ _____

Day of the Week: _____

- ☐ _____
- ☐ _____
- ☐ _____
- ☐ _____
- ☐ _____
- ☐ _____

Day of the Week: _____

- ☐ _____
- ☐ _____
- ☐ _____
- ☐ _____
- ☐ _____
- ☐ _____

# Journal

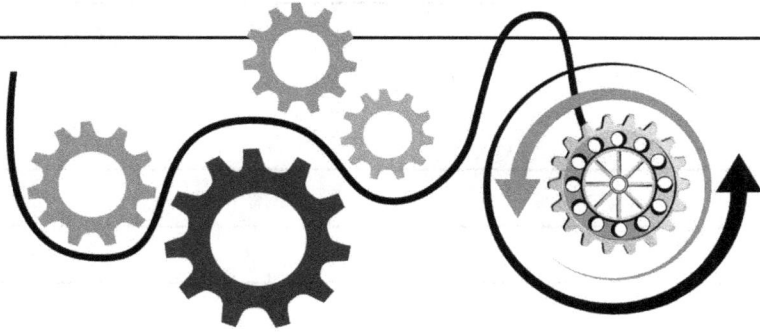

## What I Accomplished This Week

## What I Will Get To Next Week

# A Recap of My Week

The best part of my week: _____

_____

_____

_____

_____

### 5 Things I Learned This Week

○ _____

○ _____

○ _____

○ _____

○ _____

### 5 Things I Can Do To Be More Productive

○ _____

○ _____

○ _____

○ _____

○ _____

### 5 Things I'm Grateful For

○ _____

○ _____

○ _____

○ _____

○ _____

# Doodle - Brainstorm - Daydream

*"Productivity is a relative matter. And it's really insignificant:*
*What is ultimately important is a writer's strongest books."*
*—Joyce Carol Oates*

# My Main Focus for the Week of:_____

A Project I'll Be Focusing on This Week is: _____
_____
_____
_____

Why It's Important for Me to Focus on This Project This Week: _____
_____
_____
_____

## Master To-Do List for This Project

☐ _____     ☐ _____
☐ _____     ☐ _____
☐ _____     ☐ _____
☐ _____     ☐ _____
☐ _____     ☐ _____
☐ _____     ☐ _____

## How I'll Reward Myself to Celebrate My Accomplishments

_____
_____
_____
_____

# Daily Six-Most-Important Things To-Do List
## Week of: _____

Notes:

Ways I'll market my book this week:

Something fun I'll do this week is:

Day of the Week: _____

- ☐ _____
- ☐ _____
- ☐ _____
- ☐ _____
- ☐ _____
- ☐ _____

Day of the Week: _____

- ☐ _____
- ☐ _____
- ☐ _____
- ☐ _____
- ☐ _____
- ☐ _____

Day of the Week: _____

- ☐ _____
- ☐ _____
- ☐ _____
- ☐ _____
- ☐ _____
- ☐ _____

Day of the Week: _____

- ☐ _____
- ☐ _____
- ☐ _____
- ☐ _____
- ☐ _____
- ☐ _____

Day of the Week: _____

- ☐ _____
- ☐ _____
- ☐ _____
- ☐ _____
- ☐ _____
- ☐ _____

# Journal

_____
_____
_____
_____
_____
_____
_____

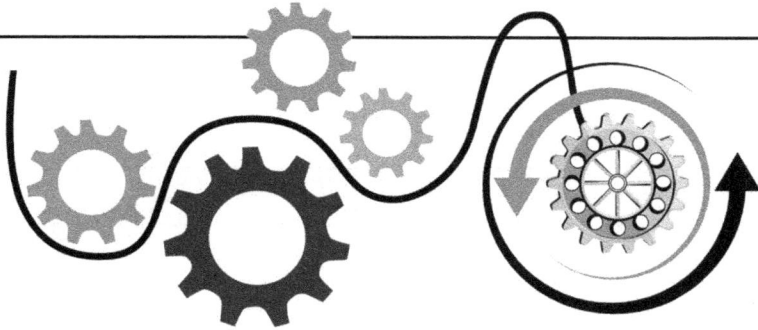

| What I Accomplished This Week | What I Will Get To Next Week |
| --- | --- |
| _____ | _____ |
| _____ | _____ |
| _____ | _____ |
| _____ | _____ |
| _____ | _____ |
| _____ | _____ |
| _____ | _____ |
| _____ | _____ |
| _____ | _____ |

# A Recap of My Week

The best part of my week: _____

_____

_____

_____

_____

### 5 Things I Learned This Week

○ _____

○ _____

○ _____

○ _____

○ _____

### 5 Things I Can Do To Be More Productive

○ _____

○ _____

○ _____

○ _____

○ _____

### 5 Things I'm Grateful For

○ _____

○ _____

○ _____

○ _____

○ _____

# Doodle - Brainstorm - Daydream

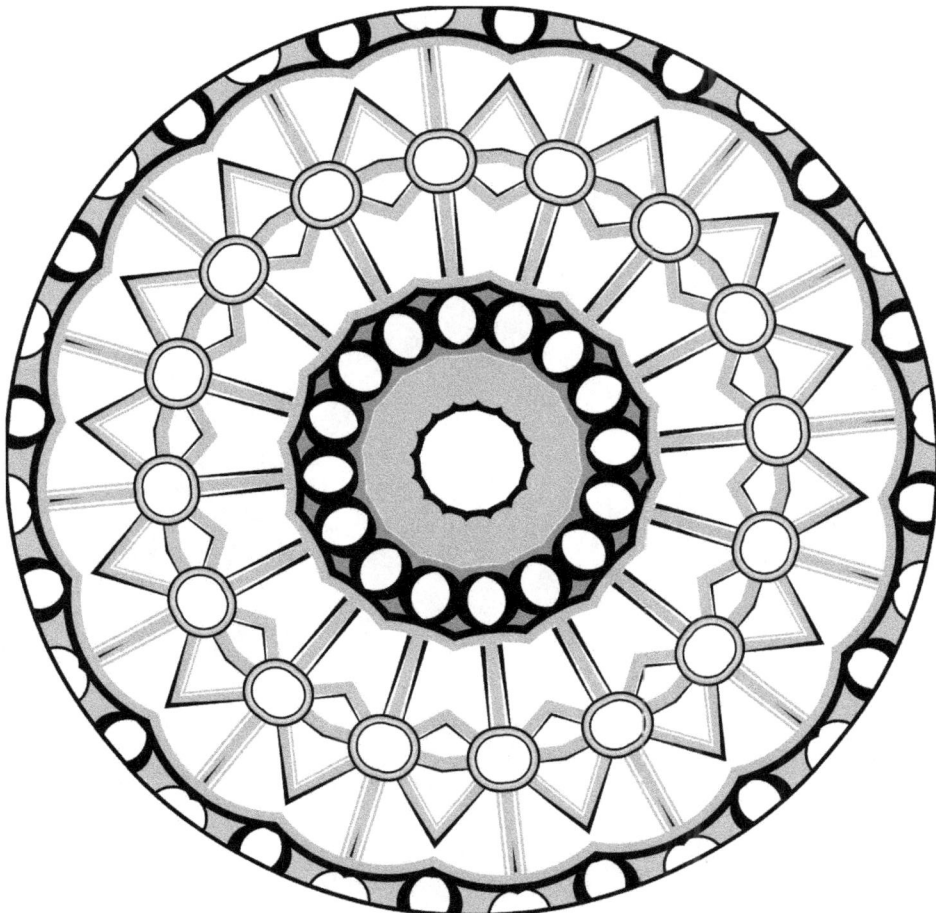

69

*"Productivity is being able to do things that you were never able to do before."*
—*Franz Kafka*

# My Main Focus for the Week of:_____

A Project I'll Be Focusing on This Week is: _____

_____

_____

_____

Why It's Important for Me to Focus on This Project This Week: _____

_____

_____

_____

## Master To-Do List for This Project

☐ _____   ☐ _____

☐ _____   ☐ _____

☐ _____   ☐ _____

☐ _____   ☐ _____

☐ _____   ☐ _____

☐ _____   ☐ _____

## How I'll Reward Myself to Celebrate My Accomplishments

_____

_____

_____

_____

# Daily Six-Most-Important Things To-Do List
## Week of: _____

| Notes: | Day of the Week: _____ |
|---|---|
| Ways I'll market my book this week: | ☐ _____ |
| | ☐ _____ |
| | ☐ _____ |
| Something fun I'll do this week is: | ☐ _____ |
| | ☐ _____ |
| | ☐ _____ |

Day of the Week: _____

☐ _____
☐ _____
☐ _____
☐ _____
☐ _____
☐ _____

Day of the Week: _____

☐ _____
☐ _____
☐ _____
☐ _____
☐ _____
☐ _____

Day of the Week: _____

☐ _____
☐ _____
☐ _____
☐ _____
☐ _____
☐ _____

Day of the Week: _____

☐ _____
☐ _____
☐ _____
☐ _____
☐ _____
☐ _____

# Journal

_____
_____
_____
_____
_____
_____
_____

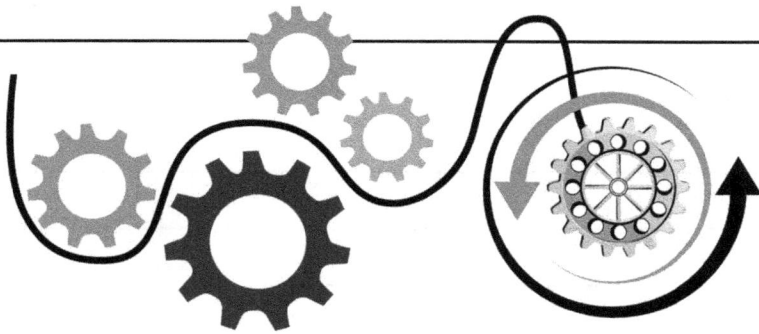

| What I Accomplished This Week | What I Will Get To Next Week |
| --- | --- |
| _____ | _____ |
| _____ | _____ |
| _____ | _____ |
| _____ | _____ |
| _____ | _____ |
| _____ | _____ |
| _____ | _____ |
| _____ | _____ |
| _____ | _____ |

# A Recap of My Week

The best part of my week: _____

_____

_____

_____

_____

### 5 Things I Learned This Week

○ _____
○ _____
○ _____
○ _____
○ _____

### 5 Things I Can Do To Be More Productive

○ _____
○ _____
○ _____
○ _____
○ _____

### 5 Things I'm Grateful For

○ _____
○ _____
○ _____
○ _____
○ _____

# Doodle - Brainstorm - Daydream

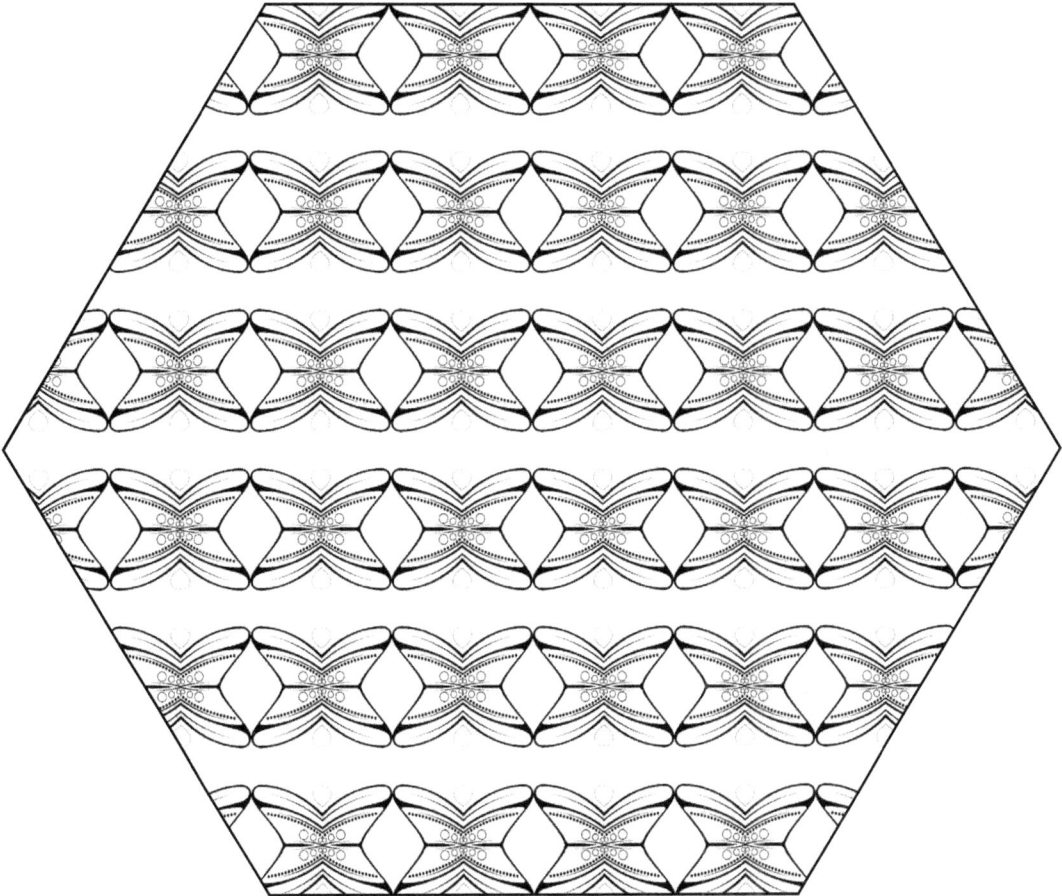

*"Aerodynamically, the bumble bee shouldn't be able to fly, but the bumble bee doesn't know it so it goes on flying anyway."*
*—Mary Kay Ash*

# Month Three Section

# Notes

## Things to Focus on This Coming Month

Month: _____ Year: _____

My #1 most important success-focused goal for this month is: _____

_____

_____

_____

_____

Why I want to acheive this goal: _____

_____

_____

_____

_____

What my life will be like when I achieve this goal: _____

_____

_____

_____

_____

How my achieving this goal will impact others: _____

_____

_____

_____

_____

# Ways I Can Improve

What I commit to doing more of: _____

_____

_____

_____

_____

What I need to let go of: _____

_____

_____

_____

_____

What I need to do differently: _____

_____

_____

_____

_____

_____

# Monthly Calendar for: Month:_____ Year:_____

(Fill in the dates for this month then plug in tasks, events, and activities.)

| Monday | Tuesday | Wednesday | Thursday | Friday |
|--------|---------|-----------|----------|--------|
|        |         |           |          |        |
|        |         |           |          |        |
|        |         |           |          |        |
|        |         |           |          |        |
|        |         |           |          |        |

# My Brain Dump Page

### For the Month of: _____ Year: _____

| Business ASAP List | Personal ASAP List | Current Main Project |
| --- | --- | --- |
| Speaking Activities | Writing Projects | Marketing Activities |
| Reading List | Courses to Study | To-Do Someday Maybe |

# My Brain Dump Page for a Specific Project

Project Description: _____

_____

# Notes

# Weekly Section for Month Three

# My Main Focus for the Week of:_____

A Project I'll Be Focusing on This Week is: _____

_____

_____

_____

Why It's Important for Me to Focus on This Project This Week: _____

_____

_____

_____

## Master To-Do List for This Project

☐ _____    ☐ _____

☐ _____    ☐ _____

☐ _____    ☐ _____

☐ _____    ☐ _____

☐ _____    ☐ _____

☐ _____    ☐ _____

## How I'll Reward Myself to Celebrate My Accomplishments

_____

_____

_____

_____

# Daily Six-Most-Important Things To-Do List
## Week of: _____

| | |
|---|---|
| **Notes:**<br><br><br>Ways I'll market my book this week:<br><br><br>Something fun I'll do this week is: | **Day of the Week:** _____<br><br>☐ _____<br>☐ _____<br>☐ _____<br>☐ _____<br>☐ _____<br>☐ _____ |
| **Day of the Week:** _____<br><br>☐ _____<br>☐ _____<br>☐ _____<br>☐ _____<br>☐ _____<br>☐ _____ | **Day of the Week:** _____<br><br>☐ _____<br>☐ _____<br>☐ _____<br>☐ _____<br>☐ _____<br>☐ _____ |
| **Day of the Week:** _____<br><br>☐ _____<br>☐ _____<br>☐ _____<br>☐ _____<br>☐ _____<br>☐ _____ | **Day of the Week:** _____<br><br>☐ _____<br>☐ _____<br>☐ _____<br>☐ _____<br>☐ _____<br>☐ _____ |

# Journal

_____
_____
_____
_____
_____
_____
_____

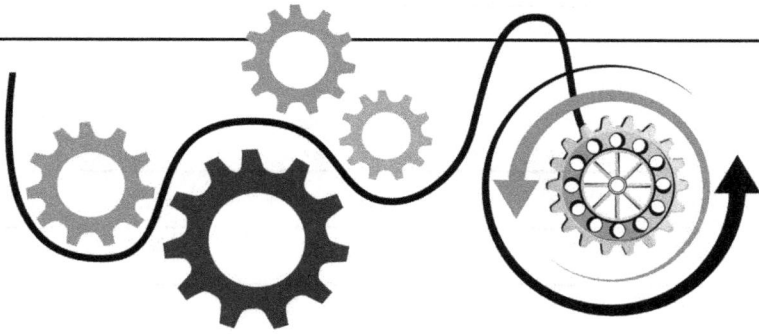

| What I Accomplished This Week | What I Will Get To Next Week |
| --- | --- |
| _____ | _____ |
| _____ | _____ |
| _____ | _____ |
| _____ | _____ |
| _____ | _____ |
| _____ | _____ |
| _____ | _____ |
| _____ | _____ |
| _____ | _____ |

# A Recap of My Week

The best part of my week: _____
_____
_____
_____
_____

### 5 Things I Learned This Week

- ○ _____
- ○ _____
- ○ _____
- ○ _____
- ○ _____

### 5 Things I Can Do To Be More Productive

- ○ _____
- ○ _____
- ○ _____
- ○ _____
- ○ _____

### 5 Things I'm Grateful For

- ○ _____
- ○ _____
- ○ _____
- ○ _____
- ○ _____

# Doodle - Brainstorm - Daydream

*"Setting goals is the first step in turning the invisible into the visible."*
—*Tony Robbins*

# My Main Focus for the Week of:_____

A Project I'll Be Focusing on This Week is: _____

_____

_____

_____

Why It's Important for Me to Focus on This Project This Week: _____

_____

_____

_____

## Master To-Do List for This Project

☐ _____    ☐ _____

☐ _____    ☐ _____

☐ _____    ☐ _____

☐ _____    ☐ _____

☐ _____    ☐ _____

☐ _____    ☐ _____

## How I'll Reward Myself to Celebrate My Accomplishments

_____

_____

_____

_____

# Daily Six-Most-Important Things To-Do List
## Week of: _____

| | |
|---|---|
| **Notes:**<br><br>Ways I'll market my book this week:<br><br><br>Something fun I'll do this week is: | **Day of the Week:** _____<br><br>☐ _____<br>☐ _____<br>☐ _____<br>☐ _____<br>☐ _____<br>☐ _____ |
| **Day of the Week:** _____<br><br>☐ _____<br>☐ _____<br>☐ _____<br>☐ _____<br>☐ _____<br>☐ _____ | **Day of the Week:** _____<br><br>☐ _____<br>☐ _____<br>☐ _____<br>☐ _____<br>☐ _____<br>☐ _____ |
| **Day of the Week:** _____<br><br>☐ _____<br>☐ _____<br>☐ _____<br>☐ _____<br>☐ _____<br>☐ _____ | **Day of the Week:** _____<br><br>☐ _____<br>☐ _____<br>☐ _____<br>☐ _____<br>☐ _____<br>☐ _____ |

# Journal

_____
_____
_____
_____
_____
_____

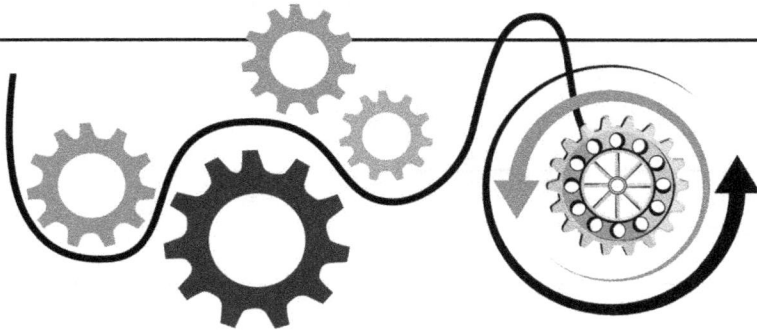

| What I Accomplished This Week | What I Will Get To Next Week |
|---|---|
| _____ | _____ |
| _____ | _____ |
| _____ | _____ |
| _____ | _____ |
| _____ | _____ |
| _____ | _____ |
| _____ | _____ |
| _____ | _____ |
| _____ | _____ |

# A Recap of My Week

The best part of my week: _____

_____

_____

_____

_____


### 5 Things I Learned This Week

○ _____

○ _____

○ _____

○ _____

○ _____


### 5 Things I Can Do To Be More Productive

○ _____

○ _____

○ _____

○ _____

○ _____


### 5 Things I'm Grateful For

○ _____

○ _____

○ _____

○ _____

○ _____

# Doodle - Brainstorm - Daydream

## TAKE TIME TO SMELL THE ROSES

*"The biggest adventure you can take is to live the life of your dreams."*
—*Oprah Winfrey*

# My Main Focus for the Week of:_____

A Project I'll Be Focusing on This Week is: _____

_____

_____

_____

Why It's Important for Me to Focus on This Project This Week: _____

_____

_____

_____

## Master To-Do List for This Project

☐ _____  ☐ _____

☐ _____  ☐ _____

☐ _____  ☐ _____

☐ _____  ☐ _____

☐ _____  ☐ _____

☐ _____  ☐ _____

## How I'll Reward Myself to Celebrate My Accomplishments

_____

_____

_____

_____

# Daily Six-Most-Important Things To-Do List
## Week of: _____

| Notes: | Day of the Week: _____ |
|---|---|
| | ☐_____ |
| Ways I'll market my book this week: | ☐_____ |
| | ☐_____ |
| | ☐_____ |
| Something fun I'll do this week is: | ☐_____ |
| | ☐_____ |

| Day of the Week: _____ | Day of the Week: _____ |
|---|---|
| ☐_____ | ☐_____ |
| ☐_____ | ☐_____ |
| ☐_____ | ☐_____ |
| ☐_____ | ☐_____ |
| ☐_____ | ☐_____ |
| ☐_____ | ☐_____ |

| Day of the Week: _____ | Day of the Week: _____ |
|---|---|
| ☐_____ | ☐_____ |
| ☐_____ | ☐_____ |
| ☐_____ | ☐_____ |
| ☐_____ | ☐_____ |
| ☐_____ | ☐_____ |
| ☐_____ | ☐_____ |

100

# Journal

_____

_____

_____

_____

_____

_____

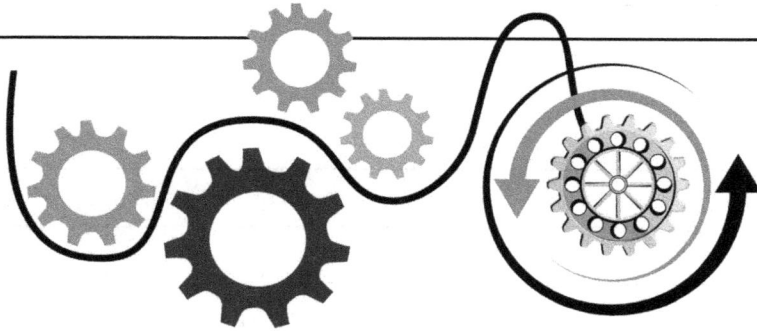

| What I Accomplished This Week | What I Will Get To Next Week |
|---|---|
| _____ | _____ |
| _____ | _____ |
| _____ | _____ |
| _____ | _____ |
| _____ | _____ |
| _____ | _____ |
| _____ | _____ |
| _____ | _____ |
| _____ | _____ |

# A Recap of My Week

The best part of my week: _____

_____

_____

_____

_____

### 5 Things I Learned This Week

○ _____

○ _____

○ _____

○ _____

○ _____

### 5 Things I Can Do To Be More Productive

○ _____

○ _____

○ _____

○ _____

○ _____

### 5 Things I'm Grateful For

○ _____

○ _____

○ _____

○ _____

○ _____

# Doodle - Brainstorm - Daydream

*"Today you are you! That is truer than true!*
*There is no one alive who is you-er than you!"*
—Dr. Seuss

# My Main Focus for the Week of: _____

A Project I'll Be Focusing on This Week is: _____

_____

_____

_____

Why It's Important for Me to Focus on This Project This Week: _____

_____

_____

_____

## Master To-Do List for This Project

- ☐ _____
- ☐ _____
- ☐ _____
- ☐ _____
- ☐ _____
- ☐ _____

- ☐ _____
- ☐ _____
- ☐ _____
- ☐ _____
- ☐ _____
- ☐ _____

## How I'll Reward Myself to Celebrate My Accomplishments

_____

_____

_____

_____

# Daily Six-Most-Important Things To-Do List
## Week of: _____

| | |
|---|---|
| Notes:<br><br>Ways I'll market my book this week:<br><br><br>Something fun I'll do this week is: | Day of the Week: _____<br><br>☐ _____<br>☐ _____<br>☐ _____<br>☐ _____<br>☐ _____<br>☐ _____ |
| Day of the Week: _____<br><br>☐ _____<br>☐ _____<br>☐ _____<br>☐ _____<br>☐ _____<br>☐ _____ | Day of the Week: _____<br><br>☐ _____<br>☐ _____<br>☐ _____<br>☐ _____<br>☐ _____<br>☐ _____ |
| Day of the Week: _____<br><br>☐ _____<br>☐ _____<br>☐ _____<br>☐ _____<br>☐ _____<br>☐ _____ | Day of the Week: _____<br><br>☐ _____<br>☐ _____<br>☐ _____<br>☐ _____<br>☐ _____<br>☐ _____ |

# Journal

_____
_____
_____
_____
_____
_____
_____

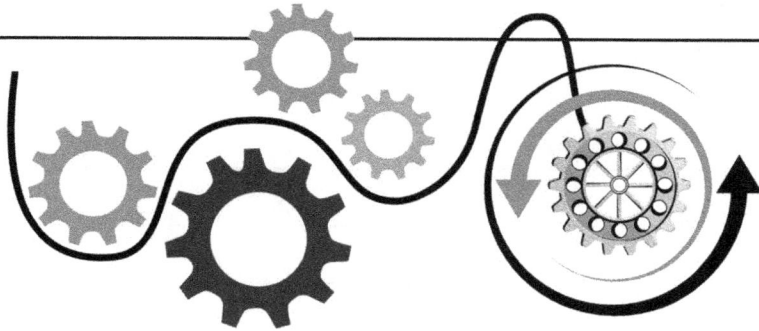

| What I Accomplished This Week | What I Will Get To Next Week |
|---|---|
| | |
| | |
| | |
| | |
| | |
| | |
| | |
| | |
| | |

# A Recap of My Week

The best part of my week: _____

_____

_____

_____

_____

### 5 Things I Learned This Week

○ _____
○ _____
○ _____
○ _____
○ _____

### 5 Things I Can Do To Be More Productive

○ _____
○ _____
○ _____
○ _____
○ _____

### 5 Things I'm Grateful For

○ _____
○ _____
○ _____
○ _____
○ _____

# Doodle - Brainstorm - Daydream

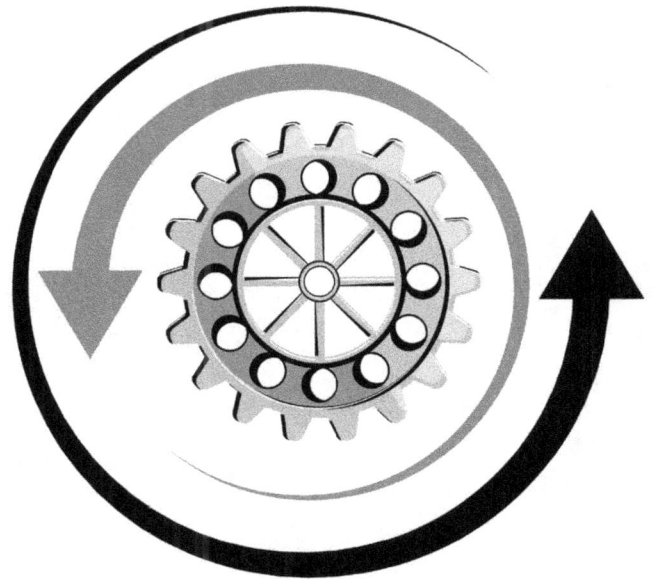

*"If you always do what you've always done, then you'll always have what you've always had."*
—*Unknown*

# Notes

# About D'vorah

D'vorah Lansky, M.Ed., is the bestselling author of several books including; *Book Marketing Made Easy: Simple Strategies for Selling Your Nonfiction Book* Online.

Having been online since 1994, D'vorah specializes in teaching authors how to market their books and grow their following, online.

D'vorah has taught thousands of authors across the globe, how to reach more readers and sell more books using online technology and relationship marketing strategies.

# What Authors Are Saying

*"D'vorah, you are the kind of leader I always wanted – but never had. Had you been the CEO where I worked, I would not have opted for self-employment. You are the kind of leader who's sorely lacking in this world, yet desperately needed. I couldn't ask for a better role model than you. I offer deep gratitude for having found you!"*
—Janine Moore, www.WorkOnYourOwnTerms.com

*"D'vorah's programs have skyrocketed my writing career to a whole new level! Through the application of the skills gained, I have seen my level of professionalism, my social media status, and my sales go through the roof! D'vorah is a light in the dark and should be commended for her customer service, attention to detail, and personal development skills!"*
—Sara Hathaway, www.AuthorSaraFHathaway.com